I0755915

FINISHING LINE PRESS
www.finishinglinepress.com

a sky with two moons

by

suzanne simons

Finishing Line Press
Georgetown, Kentucky

a sky with two moons

ISBN 979-8-89990-397-7 First Edition

Publisher: Leah Huete de Maines
Editor: Christen Kincaid
Cover Art: NASA and designer Lee Miller. Photo of Mars with its two moons, Phobos and Deimos.
Author Photo: Kelly Smith-Simons
Cover Design: Lee Miller and Elizabeth Maines McCleavy

Order online: www.finishinglinepress.com
also available on amazon.com

Author inquiries and mail orders:
Finishing Line Press
PO Box 1626
Georgetown, Kentucky 40324
USA

contents

we were overtaken by dark in strange woods, but we did not get lost.

thomas merton

for beau montana and owen maverick, and to all of your generation that you may dream, and experience the awe and wonders of the heavens.

night sky

after rebecca elson

among stars we float in a quiet in-between
entranced by their light, comforted by
swirls of galaxies. a universe of mysteries

join the lineage of astronomers-poets-mystics
gather, heave great fistfuls of stars
write with the beauty and clarity of a sparkling night sky

rice paper night at new moon

row the boat in water calm
night a friend soothing balm
drift to an open space
starry messengers sprinkle grace
midnight blue and golden stars
rock the wooden boat and oars
dip in water open faced
inky blackness thick to taste

i.

where is everybody? enrico fermi asked, on hearing an eerily quiet radio frequency in deep space

a little violet wiggle among staunch spectral lines.

*

a woman on a bus speaks to no one and everyone about beauty, magic, the soul.

*

pink geraniums spill from clay pots on the front porch.

*

a tv astronomer describes the spring sky and brilliance of mars, shining ferociously.

*

we see only about two percent of what's going on.

*

windows open inward.

first color pictures from another planet, 1965

a long time ago when the world was black and white
before dark chocolate and the Internet were a thing, a cadre of (mostly)
(white) men with
crew cuts and a couple beehived women—jet propulsion lab control
room team—

duck out to woolworth's, buy pastels of burnt sienna, mauve, russet.
ecstatic and impatient, they can't wait the hours for mariner
4 pictures of mars to be processed.

golly, they color-code the data like a paint-by-numbers set.
heck, they are spot on, confirmed by pictures of landscape like jordan.
imagine—getting to play with color after plotting logarithms,

jowling yellow #2 pencils for years. not looking for the glee of color, but a
klondike of dreams—and
look what made them happy. back here, ducklings like egg yolks embark
on their

maiden voyage across a small lake, in tow behind their mother.
neath the 5th ave. bridge, clumps of jellyfish turn water the color
of moonglow. a friend lets her hair go silver, wears frosted

pink lipstick and a cherry miniskirt. at a nearby bistro, voices of
burgundy, smoky blue
quietly inhabit a corner table.
really, life is color. the difference between staid and breath.

surely the world(s) didn't have to form this way, with flowers growing in
monet
tableaux and rainbows still giving us pause
under every type of rain. "free," the cardboard sign says i find by a curb,

venture to bring home a pink plastic table-top christmas tree with
white lights to make my bedroom pretty. mariner 4
x-terminated by micro-meteroids,

yet lasts longer than expected as a
zephyr carries whispers of awe from earth.

on naming pluto's first moon for my wife

telescopes need the heavens like i
need you. a thin shift in dots
from one night to the next,

like touching toes
then pinkies as we drift
to sleep. no moon, then one.

those dots a delicate pattern,
honey, like the constellations
of freckles on your back.

a new world with ice cliffs
four miles high, light that does
not scatter. astonishing. i loved you

before the collision
that birthed this small world
of smooth silver skin, changing

to ruddy at the north pole.
a funny shape, more potato
than orange. a bit odd,

as love is. i wanted to surprise,
name the moon for you, babe.
i consulted a dictionary,

found you also ferry souls
across the river styx.
That long night, waiting

for the learned astronomers'
decree, i could barely sleep,
nestled in close orbit with you.

ii.

imagine a sky with two moons

a gold shaft of light pierces a hole in mountain fog, shimmers a deer bronze.

*

a deaf man wins a dance contest.

*

a painting with sky the color of salmon flesh.

*

a cloud of bees on a blooming california lilac, periwinkle a verb.

*

you fix snags in my prayer shawl by stretching the yarn.

*

art of an ordinary day.

dark matter

after abdelrahman waberi

a young bald eagle, still
mottled brown, circles
slow and keen
over a wetland.
croaks of bullfrogs lace
the moist air.
a doe and yearling
graze at the edge
of a tangy green field.
a small chestnut
and white feather drift
casually into the pocket
of my heart
accelerate expansion
of the universe

cosmic inflation

you ignite
from watery bliss,
combust in a flash of heat
fusing present, future and past.
stars form out of darkness and cradle you.
the heart comes first. then, toenails, dimples,
the divot between your nose and upper lip. you expand
to the sinewy limits of blood and flesh, hear and speak in ways I do not
understand as you recombine, accelerate, even out, emerge to tend your
tiny lighthouse.

ode to numbers

in the fuzzy qualitative world
of tangles and snares, ruptures and repairs

you stand out for your crisp
clear edges, pointed storytelling

no-nonsense beauty on the limits
of the golden ratio, and your palaces

of fractals. on a sleepless night counting
gratitudes from a to z, i find solace

and joy in you alone, assurance that 1+1= 2
and sometimes 3 and 4, that no matter

how much we scorch the earth, light still
travels 186,000 miles per second, that regardless

of how many refugees we help create, pi
unfolds into an infinity of heavenly reason.

iii.

light and dark, constants in the universe. they're how we know stuff

relationships as sanctuaries.

*

mom's letter to the editor, thanking workers for the wildflowers along state highways.

*

*

a goldfinch collects thistles til her mouth was so full she had whiskers.

*

*

*

smell of pine resin in a dry forest.

*

* * *

*

*

taste of cold milk.

mercury, at last

forty years of dazzling discoveries
passed before i was interested
in seeing you more closely than a glimpse
at twilight. your big draw, neglect.

too close to the sun, too difficult
to extract your secrets. i circled you,
celestial messenger, after plundering
my own nightingales. of planets visible

to the naked eye, you are the most
illusive. to wrap myself around you
would mean death by melting.
most surprising, your magnetic field.

no one else in our inner circle has this,
just thee and me, the ability to deflect danger.

deep impact on tempel 1

deep impact—a nasa probe and first satellite
to crash land on a comet, tempel 1.

you blamed my kind for your misfortunes—
ships' captains erring course, deaths
of benevolent rulers, imbalance of yin

and yang. in a human lifetime you made me
an honored winged messenger,
then demon god of the underworld.

the year earth passed through my sister's tail,
mark twain and a whole lot more died.
the foolish grabbed anti-comet pills

and umbrellas. nowadays, what you
don't understand you smash. atoms, godzilla…
you strike, penetrate, probe me.

mark your territory with deep impact,
sear a crater into my heart that spews
fire from dust into a cobalt sky.

yet i am more delicate than a moth
or powder snow, held together
by gravity and the smell of impending rain.

mid-way on the long journey
from the outer solar system,
i replenish my core with mystery.

i cannot speak of misery.
such predictability is yours.
born of the oort cloud, i was christened

by the sun. ever since, when i grow
larger, more beautiful and move
toward brilliance, you grow volatile.

eventually, i will evaporate. for now, i remain
pitch black, the dark holding my heat.
yet through your tiny eyes,

i appear white, as everything does.

john glenn returns to space

loss of muscle and bone, balance,
sleep disrupted. hallmarks
of space flight and aging. my, oh my,
love and space, still beautiful at this age.

you wake me gently, sing
a few bars of moon river in my ear.
we spoon, your warm breath wraps
around my bare shoulders.

australia below. bathed in darkness.
except perth, which turned on the lights
for me as i orbit overhead, just like
in the hours of friendship and godspeed.

like nothing i've ever known.
why does love take so long,
and with so many missteps?

i never tire of looking at you,
earth, caressed in blues,
whites, greens and browns.

before you, i almost gave up.
with you, i gave in
to the great mystery

of space, time, knowing.

everyday rituals—

our palms cupped
on morning walks,
making your tea extra hot
with the honey that you are
re-entry not so many g's this time.

iv.

deneb, north star on mars

nest cavities, burrows and other protected spaces.

*   *   *
          *   *

whisps of summer linger on the night air.

*   **   ***

orange, lemon and lime chiffon scarves drape a neighbor's garden.

*   *   *

women poets around a table, bringing our best words.

when pluto was demoted

from planet, the international astronomical union
set new criteria for what a planet is: round
with an elliptical orbit and no serendipitous
wanderings. a planet must have cleared
its neighborhood of undesirable objects,
and preferably have moons so we can swoon
and write ample ekphrastic poetry. when pluto
was demoted, our own planet diminished.

clyde tombaugh's painstaking search
night after frigid high desert night
comparing photographic star plates declared
insignificant. textbooks rewritten, teachers retrained.
children with no memory of pluto make cut-outs
of the solar system's now eight planets, hang them
with string twirling from classroom ceilings.
my father's 1929 encyclopedia accurate again.

we forget, no longer look outward
beyond the asteroid belt for a half-sister planet
with a crazy orbit dancing over neptune.
only dwarf planets, pluto, eris and the like,
play at the outer edges of the known solar system,
in line behind gas giants. the international astronomical union,
emboldened by victory over pluto, set sights on earth.

astrophysicists detect gravitational waves for the first time

> *"we can detect new cosmic phenomenon and piece*
> *together a fresh narrative of the physics of stars in their*
> *death throes,"*
> france cordova, national science foundation director, 2014-2020

alchemy flows through the universe
wraps around neutron stars causes
them to collide in a blitz of light

sending ripples of gravity outward
like waves on a celestial ocean. the collapse
of these smallest, densest stars creates

gold and platinum. force spews the gems
to reach even earth. we do not see
any of this in the moment, but a billion

years later. how strange, death creating
beauty, even something of value we
can't see at the time, but with time.

chinese land probe on dark side of moon

> *probe: a slender, blunt surgical instrument for exploring a wound.*
> webster's dictionary

chang'e floats on a silk road of magpies,
sets down in a puff of lunar dust and silver ripples,
strews moon pebbles. from fly-bys we named
parts of our dark side—pavlov, hendrix, love—

but never fully explored her. what if the u.s.
and china split the moon down the middle?
americans get the sea of tranquility,
unfaded american flags, moon rovers

that may still work, blueprints to explode
an atom bomb while the chinese get the largest
crater for cutting veins and tissue to plant potatoes,
propagate silkworms, mine material for nuclear fusion.

on a languid summer evening, an owl glides low
into the fir trees by a hospital where life ends,
and begins. a hummingbird full and round flits like
a bumblebee across my face, hovers at the lip

of an azalea blossom. the moon gently rocks back
and forth like a globe on a dark sea. touches of earthshine
reveal some of her dark side. so does scraping the surface
where crust is thinnest. we discover the dark side

is not really dark, just far. still, we can never
see her fully, know how long and deep to bore.

v.

space between words

“my family were republicans,” raphael says in low tones over pad thai. “so were mine,” i whisper back.

**

a young convenience store clerk writes by hand in fine, ornate script directions to the magic beach hotel for me late one night.

****

a cello player peruses the poetry section of a small midwest public library, light in her eyes.

******

geese in formation traverse a silent winter night sky, too high for us to hear the flapping of wings.

mysteries

we don't know for sure
why dinosaurs went extinct,
but there are theories…
volcanoes, meteorites,
young taking too long
to hatch. we don't know
when the seed of a first kiss,
how long to germination.
as sure and unlikely as
a friendship between
crow and mourning dove,
both curious about the other
as they share a high electrical wire,
we do know a first kiss ends
in a last(ing) kiss, and in between
what makes light and heat.

from *a book of delights*

surely we include the wow! signal—6equj5—
a loud hello bobbing in a sea of zeros

and ones on a 1977 computer tape
from a radio telescope pointed at deep space.

six—mother of numbers and community,
a sign of life, skylisteners hoped.

no repeat since. in the dreamspace of time
maybe the signal will come again.

why do we keep searching? maybe
we want to lightly brush the big bang's

first whisper, or the stardust of our own origins,
for kindred life who will teach us a better way

to be. or we hope to find the mystic force of love,
that river of energy igniting every speck

of interstellar dust, spark of star shine, swirl of galaxies.
maybe we're really looking for God.

murmurs of earth

to the makers of music—all worlds, all time.
inscription on the golden record of earth
sounds and images aboard voyager 1,
somewhere beyond our solar system.

a footstep, a heartbeat, a kiss.

greetings to our friends in the stars.
we wish that we will meet you someday,"
an arabic greeting on this gestalt of language
and sounds lacquered in uranium, its half-life
stretching into a future farther than all our pasts.

a kiss, a footstep, a heartbeat.

we greet you, great ones. we wish you
longevity, a nguni hello.
we hope we are not alone,
that we find each other,
embrace a million lifetimes.

a heartbeat, a footfall.

"friends from space, how are you all?
have you eaten yet? come visit us if you
have time," an amoy blessing. like laughter
and licking, a scan of ann druyen's brain waves
still dancing two days after carl sagan proposed.

a kiss.

indian raga, navajo night chant,
johnny b. goode. a mother breastfeeds,
bonded in gaze with her child, an x-ray
of hands, a whale singing. *welcome home.*
it is a pleasure to receive you, a punjab welcome.

a heartbeat.

pronoia

peering through gas and dust,
radio telescopes hear the unseen—
thrumming corpses of pulsars, clicks

of black holes. we hear clearly
when we listen together, all pointed
at the same mystery patch of heaven.

pythagoras believed only gods heard
the music of the spheres. plato claimed
sirens sang in harmony from each planet.

a team of astronomers from around
the world points dishes of ears
to collectively take the first picture

of a black hole. bats, dolphins see by sound.
we do too, sometimes. raindrops land thickly
on rooftops after weeks without rain.

girlfriends belly laugh around a game
of skip bo. Ballpark announcers boom glee
at the smack of a home run. say yes.

arecibo! arriba! je t'adore!

faith

after david whyte

i want to have faith

that earth will right herself
from our inflictions,
that gravity will hold us
together.

so i look to the heavens
for good order, predictable laws,
pinpricks of light against utter
darkness.

what if life is everywhere?

the wise astronomers
say it's likely, that evidence
surrounds us—

fossils on a martian meteor,
the deepest of oceans
with heat vents under ice
on a moon of saturn,
the heart of pluto.

imagine, no longer feeling alone.

we may be here
because jupiter wobbled,
destroying earth's dinosaurs
with the flick of an asteroid.

we may be here
because our neighborhood
in the galaxy has matured
beyond rocky chunks
of proto-planets and their
terrible impacts.

we may be here
because we still have faith.

eclipse of a supermoon

we've seen pictures of the moon turning
the color of a martian desert.

we know it will be as full as a mother
about to give birth, and exactly what time

the faintest sliver will levitate
just above the horizon.

we don't know we will forget
that which is not quite surprise

or mystery, but like nothing
we've ever seen. that on this dark night

we'll heat leftover meatloaf, pour wine
from a box, settle in with reruns

of china beach. until we hear neighbors
murmur, gather on street corners

pointing their children east. we are meant
to be fulfilled on this earth, marvel

at our luminosity. on this good night,
moondrops stir thistles, replace our own umbra.

we may yet mingle as stardust

(here are some thoughts i want you to know:)

light and darkness, light and darkness. four things
in my closet that give me pleasure: a plush burgundy
bathrobe, hiking boots, grandma tillie's cherry wood
dresser, a lavender sachet.

dream journal (a roster of chicago cubs batting
900—1,000). light and darkness.

a trust-fall into the universe (applied civics).

the value of silence. [a dinner table conversation over broasted
chicken and greens: "we couldn't get the minister
to leave…he'd been there 30 years…so i joined the quakers].

like jacob of the torah, a wrestling with spirit (darkness
and light). i let myself be found.

dumb things overheard [he: "what do you do?"
she: "i'm a poet." he: "do you write?"]. light and darkness,
darkness and light.

today and tomorrow (both/and). light and darkness.
i paint with a palette knife for texture.

my four favorite celestial objects: the milky way, pleiades, moon, earth.

imnaha river nocturne

astronomical dawn. a faint glow
in the east rises toward an embroidery
of stars laced with interstellar dust,

part of the cosmic web stitching together
the entire universe. jupiter hangs surreally
large above the horizon. stars stream

from my eyes for this beauty and magnificence,
for bedouin who always knew the heavens
    and are losing sight of them,

for billions of people who have
never seen the milky way.
how will we find our way home?

pocketful of seeds

he likes flying alone, faster than superman.
the solitude and borderline trouble. orbiting the moon,
relying on himself and houston in his ear. picked to fly,
not to land. his forgotten mission to tend seeds

while the other astronauts collect rocks and shoot
golf balls between craters. he always loved nature
and risked to save it, jumping from airplanes into smoke
and flaming forests. symbiotic, space and nature.

mission accomplished, the astronauts reunite
in the command module. moonglow recedes,
earthshine grows as the good gardener and his golfers
speed home. on re-entry, the canister of 500

sycamore, redwood and loblolly pine seeds explodes
along with fears of contamination and mysterious effects
of zero gravity and radiation. the seeds prove resilient,
and moon trees and half moon trees and their descendants

sprout and still tower around and around and around earth,
lofty crowns reaching toward the stars where they were born
and nurtured, growing long after we forget
about golf balls languishing in the lunar vacuum.

vi.

wind released on earth for the first time

a surprise snow, flakes thicker than eyelashes.

*
*
*

camaraderie of cooking together.

* *

where does time go when it passes?

*
* *

the full moon hasn't rolled downhill yet.

*
*
*

peace, as old as the stars

* ***** *

visionaries

*
* *

trees at night

sentinels, they sway
creak in velvet
darkness with soft
needles, prickly pine
cones, sturdy trunks,
pulsing sap, the air
we breathe…
they soften our gaze,
gather our troubles.
from them comes
our joy and purpose.
they grow slowly,
with certainty,
uninterrupted
save for fire…
each ring a thousand
delights, sorrows
from life-giving rains
and years of ash.

embrace the trees,
especially at night.
let forests bathe,
and nourish us
in their moist wood
scents. even as
their boughs sag
with heavy snow
in deep winter
their crowns still stretch
upward, and a great tangle
of roots anchor,
spread unseen.
faithful through all
seasons…
lie still,
pause.
listen to the trees.
they always whisper
at night.

end notes

"night sky"

rebecca elson (1960-1999), canadian poet and astronomer who pioneered understanding of globular clusters.

"a little violet wiggle among spectral lines"

changes in the spectral lines of a star in the constellation pegasus led astronomers in 1995 to discover the first planet outside of our solar system. since that time, more than 3,000 exo-planets have been identified.

the planet has a four-day orbit around its sun-like star, 51 pegasus b, making it much closer to its star than mercury's 88-day orbit around our sun. the exo-planet is not a stripped core of a brown dwarf star as was suspected but a gas giant similar to jupiter, with a thick atmosphere not blown away by solar wind. the findings were incompatible with theories of planetary formation at the time, which held gas giants would be found in more distant orbits from their stars. originally named bellerophon for the rider of the winged horse pegasus in greek mythology, the name was changed to dimidium (latin for half, as in half the mass of jupiter) through a naming contest by the international astronomical union won by a swiss team.

"first color pictures from another planet, 1965"

processing color pictures of mars sent back to earth by mariner 4 took several hours. excited and impatient with anticipation to see the first color pictures from mars, the jet propulsion lab ground crew rushed out and bought colored pencils, and drew colors on a map of the region of mars the spacecraft had photographed that they thought would match the actual colors. they were spot on.

"on naming pluto's first moon for my wife"

charon was discovered by jim christy in 1978, which he named for his wife, char. planets and moons are typically named for mythological characters, so christy based his proposal that his wife's name was encompassed in the mythical ferryman charon, who carried souls across the river styx to the underworld. thus the international astronomical union approved christy's recommendation.

“dark matter”

thought to account for about 85 percent of matter in the universe, and about 25 percent of its total density. although its existence was long suspected, it wasn’t until the 1970s that astronomers vera rubin and w. kent ford confirmed dark matter’s existence.

“cosmic inflation”

inflation refers to the explosively rapid expansion of space-time that occurred a tiny fraction of a second after the big bang. in another fraction of a second, inflation slowed to a more leisurely expansion that continues to this day and is accelerating. the term was coined in 1980 by astrophysicist alan guth to explain conditions observed in the universe.

“mercury, at last”

a 1973 fly-by by of mercury by mariner 10 mapped half the planet’s surface, and discovered a thin atmosphere of hydrogen and helium, and poles cold enough for ice. most surprising was an unexpected magnetic field similar to earth’s—neither venus, mars or our moon has one. mercury is the most difficult of the naked-eye inner planets to see due to its proximity to the sun. no spacecraft returned to mercury for 40 years, making it the least explored inner planet.

mariner 10 was the first spacecraft to use the slingshot effect of another planet’s gravity, in this case venus’, to reach its destination. the process was a test that has been successfully used in space probe exploration of the outer planets.

“deep impact on tempel 1”

on July 4, 2005, the nasa probe deep impact became the first satellite to crash land on a comet, tempel 1. the impact created a crater, and allowed scientists to study first-hand the composition of a comet, and links to the origin of our solar system. deep impact established that comets have the density of powder snow, appear white but are actually black, and are held together by gravity and olfactory molecules.

the probe was preceded in 1986 by six fly-bys of halley’s comet by spacecraft from the european space agency, the soviet union, and the united states.

the oort cloud, a nursery of comets, lies beyond the orbits of the outermost planets of our solar system, and from which some are dislodged when perturbed to fall toward the sun.

"john glenn returns to space"

at age 77, john glenn became the world's oldest formally trained astronaut to go to space, 37 years after he became the first american to orbit the earth in 1962. actor william shatner, commander from the original star trek tv show, rocketed into space at age 90 as part of a commercial flight.

"astrophysicists detect gravitational waves for the first time"

a billion years ago in a galaxy far away, two neutron stars collided, spewing gold and lead. in 2015, a fragment of their death throes reached earth in the form of gravitational waves, or ripples in space-time. such ripples move through galaxies, stars, and planets, demonstrating that space is elastic and can be bent, warped and squished.

for weeks following the smashup, radio and light waves were detected—x ray, ultraviolet, and infrared. neutron stars are the smallest, densest stars known and are formed when massive stars explode in supernovas. the discovery was made through a collaboration of the u.s.-based laser interferometer gravitational-wave observatory, the europe-based virgo detector, and some 70 ground-and space-based observatories around the world.

"chinese land probe on dark side of moon"

chang'e is the name of the chinese lunar probe that landed on the far side of the moon in 2019. it was the first lunar probe from any nation to do so. the name comes from a chinese legend of two lovers who had been separated and are reunited by a bridge of magpies.

u.s. flags planted on the moon in the late 1960s and early 1970s are surprisingly unfaded, though the Apollo 11 flag toppled over as the astronauts blasted off from the lunar surface to return to earth. moon rovers are still there, and the u.s. did have plans to explode an atom bomb on the moon during the cold war.

china's chang'e probe set up a greenhouse to cultivate potatoes and silkworms, as well as to determine the feasibility of mining nuclear fusion material in an area of the moon where the crust is thinnest. pavlov, hendrix, and love are craters on the dark side of the moon. the moon appears to rock back and forth slightly, revealing a sliver of the far side, due to the moon's orbital mechanics and the geometry of our perspective from earth.

"from *a book of delights*"

the "wow" signal—6equj5—was a 72-second intense, powerful radio signal received by the big ear telescope in ohio in 1977. the inexplicable series of numbers and letters so excited astronomer jerry ehman that he circled the series of letters and numbers in bright red ink and wrote "wow!" in the margin of the computer tape otherwise filled with zeroes and ones received by the telescope. theories on the origin of the signal include extraterrestrial life or the sudden brightening of a cold hydrogen cloud struck by a flare of a super-magnetized extremely dense star.

"murmurs of earth"

a 12-inch, gold-plated phonographic record—an audiovisual time capsule of the diversity of life and cultures on earth—is on board the voyager 1 spacecraft traveling beyond our solar system. the probe has continued to send data to earth since its launch in 1977.

astronomer carl sagan chaired a nasa committee to establish contents of the record. the result was 115 images and a variety of natural sounds, such as those made by surf, wind and thunder, birds, whales, and other animals. also included was a recording of sagan's fiancée ann druyen's heartbeat after he proposed to her and musical selections from a variety of cultures and eras, spoken greetings in 55 languages, and printed messages from president jimmy carter and u.n. secretary general kurt waldheim. "the spacecraft will be encountered and the record played only if there are advanced spacefaring civilizations in interstellar space, but the launching of this 'bottle' into the cosmic 'ocean' says something very hopeful about life on this planet," sagan noted.

"pronoia"

a team of 200 radio astronomers from around the world collaborated to take the first "picture" of a black hole, m 87, in 2019, combining observations from multiple radio telescopes in separate locations. a computer rendering assigned colors to the black hole "photo."

radio telescopes can be used in daylight and night, and collect radio, not optical, waves. they cut more easily through interstellar gas and dust. the first radio waves from space were detected by karl jansky in 1932.

"pocketful of seeds"

on the apollo 14 moon landing mission, stuart roosa, command module pilot and former smokejumper, orbited the moon while fellow astronauts alan shepard and edgar mitchell landed on the moon to collect rocks and shoot golf balls. part of roosa's mission was to tend 500 tree seeds, a cooperative experiment between nasa and the u.s. forest service, to determine if seeds would sprout after being exposed to zero gravity and radiation. after return to earth, almost all the seeds sprouted. some of those moon trees and their descendants still thrive today.

sources:

nasa, laser interferometer gravitational-wave observatory at caltech and mit, smithsonian magazine, astronomy magazine.

gratitude/acknowledgments

poetry is a collaborative art. It is crafted through support from family, friends and poetry peeps so that we as poets can bear witness to the people and communities, plants and animals, streams and stars and other sentient beings that we share the planet and the cosmos with. and then there are the editors, publishers and production teams who help send our poems out into the world. we truly are all connected. thank you all.

bows of gratitude also to the editors of the following publications who first launched these poems:

"rice paper night at new moon," *open books anthology*
"first color pictures from another planet, 1965," *cirque journal*
"ode to numbers," olympia, washington friends meeting newsletter
"murmurs of earth," *pensive: a global journal of spirituality & the arts*
"eclipse of a supermoon," *western friend magazine*

an award-winning journalist-turned-poet, **suzanne simons** initiated the city of olympia, washington's poet laureate program. suzanne's poems have been widely anthologized, including in *i sing the salmon home* (empty bowl press), winner of the 2024 washington state book award for best poetry. her work has also appeared in literary journals, including *issued: stories of service* and *aethlon: journal of sports literature*, and in stone at a local skateboard park. her first full-length collection is *road to winnemucca* (gorham, 2024). she earned an mfa from sierra nevada college, and was honored to work with poet and iraqi war veteran brian turner; nevada poet laureate gailmarie pahmeier; california poet laureate lee herrick; and mother of the spoken word movement patricia smith.

a sky with two moons brings suzanne close to full circle to her childhood dream of working as an astronomer. by the fourth grade, she had read all the astronomy books in the adult section of the public library, had a subscription to *sky & telescope magazine*, and delighted in star-gazing through her own wobbly tripod telescope. eventually, she veered off into journalism and academia where she reported, edited, consulted, and taught environmental and social justice through the lenses of poetry, middle east studies, community studies and journalism. she is professor emerita at the evergreen state college. suzannesimons.net

www.ingramcontent.com/pod-product-compliance
Lightning Source LLC
LaVergne TN
LVHW090538110826
845146LV00003B/1161
* 9 7 9 8 8 9 9 9 0 3 9 7 7 *